Living Baggage Free

"Workbook"

A Journey To Emotional Freedom and Healing

FAUSTA C. PHELAN

Living Baggage Free "Workbook"
Copyright © 2025 Fausta C. Phelan

Published by Skinny Brown Dog Media
Atlanta, GA / Punta del Este, Uruguay

For Information, Contact:
Distributed by Skinny Brown Dog Media
Website: https://www.skinnybrowndogmedia.com
Email: Info@SkinnyBrownDogMedia.com

To Contact the Author:
Fausta C. Phelan
Website: https://www.fcpleadtoserve.com

Library of Congress Cataloging in Publication Data
Paperback: ISBN 978-1-965235-54-6
eBook: ISBN 978-1-965235-55-3

Living Baggage Free Workbook

Welcome to the *Living Baggage Free Workbook*. I'm so excited to guide you through this transformative journey toward releasing emotional baggage and embracing a life of clarity, peace, and purpose. This workbook is designed to complement the concepts in my book, *Living Baggage Free*, by providing you with actionable exercises, reflective prompts, and practical tools to deepen your healing journey. Together, we will explore the themes from each chapter and apply them directly to your life in a meaningful way.

As you work through this guide, remember that emotional healing is a journey, not a destination. It's about peeling back layers, uncovering truths, and stepping into your full potential. Each exercise is a step forward—a moment to pause, reflect, and grow. Trust in yourself and your ability to embrace this transformation fully. You deserve to live a life unburdened by the weight of the past.

Adding a suggestion in the **"How to Use This Workbook"** section to include an explanation and recommendation for using a journal is an excellent idea. This will ensure that readers have ample space for reflection without creating unnecessary blank pages within the workbook. Here's how it could look:

Living baggage-free starts with a single choice—to let go of what no longer serves you and embrace the freedom waiting on the other side.

LIVING BAGGAGE FREE WORKBOOK THE JOURNEY AHEAD

How to Use This Workbook

Congratulations on taking the first step toward living baggage-free! This workbook is your companion on a transformative journey toward emotional freedom, resilience, and healing. Each chapter contains thought-provoking exercises, journal prompts, and visualizations designed to guide you step by step.

To get the most out of this workbook, consider the following tips:

1. **Grab a Journal**: While this workbook includes space for notes, having a dedicated journal allows you to expand on your reflections and track your growth over time.

2. **Set Aside Time**: Dedicate a quiet time each day or week to focus on the exercises. This intentional time is a gift to yourself.

3. **Be Honest**: The journey to freedom requires vulnerability and honesty. Write openly and without judgment.

4. **Celebrate Progress**: Healing is not a race. Celebrate each insight, breakthrough, and step forward.

5. **Revisit Often**: Life changes, and so do you. Return to this workbook and your journal to revisit exercises and reflect on how far you've come.

With your journal by your side and an open heart, you're ready to embark on a journey to emotional freedom and clarity. Let's get started!

TABLE OF CONTENTS

Chapter

1

Awareness is the first step toward freedom. Let's uncover the hidden burdens and start releasing them, one at a time.

IDENTIFYING EMOTIONAL BAGGAGE

Reflection and Awareness

In Chapter 1 of *Living Baggage Free*, we explore how unaddressed emotions can weigh us down, often without our conscious awareness. These burdens can influence our thoughts, decisions, and interactions in subtle but powerful ways. Recognizing your emotional baggage is the first step toward unraveling its hold on your life. Awareness brings clarity, and clarity opens the door to transformation. Let's start by identifying what you've been carrying and how it's been affecting you.

Often, we move through life without realizing how much emotional weight we're carrying. It could be unresolved conflict, lingering guilt, or even fear of failure. These hidden forces shape our perceptions and hold us back from living fully. In this chapter, you'll embark on a journey of self-discovery. Together, we'll uncover these weights and begin the important work of letting them go. Remember, identifying your baggage isn't about dwelling on the past—it's about reclaiming your future.

Exercise 1: Emotional Awareness Timeline

I invite you to create a timeline of key life events that may have contributed to your emotional baggage. Begin by marking significant moments—both positive and challenging—from childhood to the present. As you reflect on each event, consider how it has shaped your current emotional state.

Ask yourself:

1. What are the earliest experiences you remember that left a strong emotional impact?

   _____

   _____

   _____

2. Which events do you revisit in your thoughts or dreams?

   _____

   _____

   _____

3. How do these experiences influence your daily life or decision-making?

   _____

   _____

   _____

By mapping out these events, you'll start to uncover the root causes of your emotional baggage. This exercise is about gaining clarity and understanding so that we can begin the process of healing together. Remember, clarity is the first step to change.

Exercise 2: Baggage Categories

Now let's break your baggage into categories. Review the following areas and think about where you feel most burdened:

- **Family Relationships**

  _____

  _____

  _____

- **Romantic Relationships**

  _____

  _____

  _____

- **Workplace Challenges**

  _____

  _____

  _____

- **Personal Failures**

  _____

  _____

  _____

- **Unrealized Dreams**

  _____

  _____

  _____

For each category, write down specific instances or emotions you associate with it and rate the emotional weight it carries on a scale of 1 to 10. This will help you pinpoint which areas of your life are most affected by unresolved emotions and where we should focus our healing work first. Remember, this is not about judging your past but understanding it to create a healthier, more empowered future. Each category offers a glimpse into the areas of your life that need your attention and care. Let's take this step together, one piece at a time.

Exercise 3: Shifting Perspectives

Choose one event from your timeline that feels especially heavy. Let's reframe it together by answering these questions:

1. How would your best friend or someone who loves you unconditionally describe this event?

   _____

   _____

   _____

2. What strengths or lessons have you gained from this experience?

   _____

   _____

   _____

3. If you could revisit this moment, what would you tell your past self to offer comfort or clarity?

   _____

   _____

   _____

Reframing your experiences helps you uncover hidden strengths and see your journey in a new light. Even the most challenging moments can contribute to your personal growth and resilience. Every hardship holds a lesson or a strength waiting to be discovered. Together, we'll rewrite the narratives that no longer serve you

Visualization: Letting Go of a Heavy Bag

Take a moment to close your eyes and imagine holding a heavy suitcase filled with your emotional baggage. Picture yourself opening the suitcase and pulling out each item. One by one, acknowledge it, then release it. Once you've emptied the suitcase, reflect on how you feel.

This visualization exercise is a powerful way to practice letting go. You're creating space for healing and reclaiming your energy and peace of mind. Imagine the lightness and freedom you'll feel when the weight is no longer yours to carry.

Journal Prompt

Take some time to write about what emotional burdens you're ready to leave behind and what you want to embrace instead. Let this be your first step in releasing the weight of your past.

_____

_____

_____

_____

_____

Action Step

Write down one small, actionable step you'll take this week to address a piece of your emotional baggage. It could be as simple as scheduling a therapy session, starting a gratitude journal, or having a heart-to-heart conversation. Small steps lead to big changes. Let's commit to progress, not perfection.

_____

_____

_____

_____

_____

Chapter

2

What lies beneath the surface often holds us back the most.
By shining a light on the unseen, we begin to reclaim our power.

ACKNOWLEDGING THE UNSEEN BURDEN

Understanding Hidden Burdens

In Chapter 2, we explore the hidden burdens that subtly shape our lives, often operating beneath our conscious awareness. These unseen weights can emerge in subtle ways—perhaps in the form of unexplained anxiety, recurring negative thoughts, or feelings of being "stuck." When we're not aware of these influences, they continue to guide our responses, sometimes pulling us away from the life we long to live.

Recognizing Their Impact

Acknowledging these hidden burdens is an act of courage. It's about shining a light into those unseen corners of our heart and mind, bringing understanding where confusion once lived. These burdens can manifest as patterns of self-doubt, fear, or even physical tension. Recognizing their impact on your daily life is the first step toward reclaiming your power and creating space for healing.

Steps to Release Them

The process of uncovering these weights allows us to take the first steps toward releasing them, creating room for emotional clarity and growth. In this chapter, I'll guide you through exercises that will help you bring these hidden weights to the surface and gently begin the work of letting them go. Remember, this is a journey of self-compassion and discovery, not one of self-judgment.

Uncovering Hidden Emotional Weights

In Chapter 2, we explore the hidden burdens that subtly shape our lives, often operating beneath our conscious awareness. These unseen weights can emerge in subtle ways—perhaps in the form of unexplained anxiety, recurring negative thoughts, or feelings of being "stuck." When we're not aware of these influences, they continue to guide our responses, sometimes pulling us away from the life we long to live.

Acknowledging these hidden burdens is an act of courage. It's about shining a light into those unseen corners of our heart and mind, bringing understanding where confusion once lived. The process of uncovering these weights allows us to take the first steps toward releasing them, creating room for emotional clarity and growth. In this chapter, I'll guide you through exercises that will help you bring these hidden weights to the surface and gently begin the work of letting them go. Remember, this is a journey of self-compassion and discovery, not one of self-judgment.

Exercise 1: Self-Compassion Reflection

Take a moment to reflect on how you treat yourself during difficult times. Let's be honest here—sometimes, we're our own harshest critics. Write your responses to the following:

1. How do I talk to myself when I'm struggling?

    _____

    _____

    _____

2. Would I speak to a loved one the same way? Why or why not?

    _____

    _____

    _____

3. What words of kindness can I offer myself in moments of pain?

    _____

    _____

    _____

Compassion is a cornerstone of healing. Imagine a friend coming to you with the same struggles—how would you respond to them? Perhaps you'd offer a warm hug, a listening ear, or reassuring words. Now, picture giving yourself that same grace and care. For example, if you're feeling overwhelmed, remind yourself, "I'm doing my best, and that's enough." This practice can soften self-criticism and open the door to greater emotional healing.

Take a moment to reflect on how you treat yourself during difficult times. Let's be honest here—sometimes, we're our own harshest critics. Write your responses to the following:

1. How do I talk to myself when I'm struggling?

   _____

   _____

   _____

2. Would I speak to a loved one the same way? Why or why not?

   _____

   _____

   _____

3. What words of kindness can I offer myself in moments of pain?

   _____

   _____

   _____

Compassion is a cornerstone of healing. This exercise invites you to examine the inner dialogue that shapes your self-perception and cultivate a gentler, more supportive relationship with yourself.

Exercise 2: Identifying Triggers

Let's take a closer look at what sets off your emotional responses. Triggers often stem from unresolved past experiences or deeply ingrained patterns. Recognizing these triggers is critical for building emotional resilience because it helps you break the cycle of reactive behavior and fosters self-awareness.

For example, imagine feeling sudden frustration during a meeting when someone interrupts you. This trigger might stem from a childhood experience where your voice wasn't valued. By identifying this connection, you can respond with greater understanding and patience instead of letting frustration take over.

List five situations or interactions that trigger strong emotions like anger, sadness, or fear. For each trigger, explore:

1. What underlying emotion or memory might be connected to this trigger?

   _____

   _____

   _____

2. How do I usually respond, and how does it affect me?

   _____

   _____

   _____

3. What healthier response could I practice in the future?

   _____

   _____

   _____

Understanding your triggers is key to breaking reactive patterns and fostering emotional resilience. This exercise will help you identify the root causes of your reactions and develop strategies for responding more constructively.

Let's take a closer look at what sets off your emotional responses. List five situations or interactions that trigger strong emotions like anger, sadness, or fear. For each trigger, explore:

1. What underlying emotion or memory might be connected to this trigger?

_____

_____

_____

2. How do I usually respond, and how does it affect me?

_____

_____

_____

3. What healthier response could I practice in the future?

_____

_____

_____

Understanding your triggers is key to breaking reactive patterns and fostering emotional resilience. This exercise will help you identify the root causes of your reactions and develop strategies for responding more constructively.

Visualization: Releasing the Burden

Imagine carrying a heavy backpack filled with unseen burdens. Picture yourself standing in a peaceful environment—perhaps a quiet forest, a serene beach, or a cozy room filled with soft light. Take a moment to feel the weight of the backpack on your shoulders. Now, visualize opening the backpack and carefully removing each burden, one by one. As you release each item, notice its shape, color, or texture and let it float away into the air, dissolve into the ground, or disappear into the waves. Pay attention to how your body feels lighter, your breath becomes deeper, and your mind grows clearer with each release. Once the backpack is empty, imagine closing it and setting it aside, feeling a profound sense of relief and freedom. Write down how this experience made you feel and any insights you gained during the visualization.

Imagine carrying a heavy backpack filled with unseen burdens. Visualize opening the backpack and letting each burden float away, one by one. Take a deep breath and notice the lightness in your body as the weight lifts. Write down how you feel afterward.

Journal Prompt

Reflect on a time when you felt emotionally weighed down but didn't realize it. What signs or symptoms did you notice in hindsight, and how might you approach those feelings differently now? Consider both the immediate effects, such as stress or fatigue, and the long-term impact, like changes in your relationships or personal goals. How might releasing this burden create space for growth and joy in your life? Let your thoughts flow freely as you explore the transformative power of letting go.

_____

_____

_____

_____

_____

Action Step

This week, choose one small yet meaningful action to address an unseen burden you've identified. It could involve practicing self-compassion, such as writing a kind note to yourself or replacing a critical thought with a supportive one. Alternatively, focus on managing a specific trigger by pausing and practicing a new, healthier response. These steps might feel small, but each one builds resilience and moves you closer to living baggage-free. Celebrate each effort, knowing you're making progress on your journey to emotional freedom.

_____

_____

_____

_____

_____

Chapter 3

Freedom comes when we disrupt old patterns and create new, empowering narratives. Let's rewrite the story together.

BREAKING THE CYCLE OF NEGATIVITY

Understanding the Loop of Negative Patterns

In Chapter 3, we explore how negative patterns can keep us stuck in emotional and mental cycles that drain our energy and limit our growth. These patterns often stem from deep-seated beliefs or past experiences, shaping our thoughts and behaviors. Breaking free from these loops requires both awareness and intentional action. The good news? You have the power to change these patterns and rewrite your story.

Negative cycles often appear in our self-talk, relationships, or reactions to stress. Perhaps you notice a tendency to expect the worst, to overanalyze interactions, or to shy away from opportunities due to fear of failure. For example, procrastination can be a common negative pattern. You might find yourself delaying important tasks because of self-doubt, which leads to unnecessary stress and reinforces feelings of inadequacy. Recognizing these cycles is the first step toward transforming them. In this chapter, we'll work together to identify the negative patterns in your life and replace them with empowering habits and beliefs.

In Chapter 3, we explore how negative patterns can keep us stuck in emotional and mental cycles that drain our energy and limit our growth. These patterns often stem from deep-seated beliefs or past experiences, shaping our thoughts and behaviors. Breaking free from these loops requires both awareness and intentional action. The good news? You have the power to change these patterns and rewrite your story.

Negative cycles often appear in our self-talk, relationships, or reactions to stress. Perhaps you notice a tendency to expect the worst, to overanalyze interactions, or to shy away from opportunities due to fear of failure. Recognizing these cycles is the first step toward transforming them. In this chapter, we'll work together to identify the negative patterns in your life and replace them with empowering habits and beliefs.

Exercise 1: Pattern Recognition

Take some time to reflect on areas where you feel "stuck." Write your responses to the following:

1. What recurring thoughts or beliefs seem to hold you back?

   _____

   _____

   _____

2. How do these thoughts influence your actions and decisions?

   _____

   _____

   _____

3. When did you first notice these patterns?

   _____

   _____

   _____

4. Consider specific areas of your life, such as work, relationships, or self-care. Are there recurring themes in these areas that point to deeper patterns?

_____

_____

_____

By identifying these patterns, we're taking a significant step toward breaking free from them. Awareness is the catalyst for change.

Take some time to reflect on areas where you feel "stuck." Write your responses to the following:

1. What recurring thoughts or beliefs seem to hold you back?

_____

_____

_____

2. How do these thoughts influence your actions and decisions?

_____

_____

_____

3. When did you first notice these patterns?

_____

_____

_____

By identifying these patterns, we're taking a significant step toward breaking free from them. Awareness is the catalyst for change.

Exercise 2: Rewriting the Narrative

Choose one negative thought pattern and explore how you can reframe it. Answer the following:

1. What is the evidence for and against this thought?

    _____

    _____

    _____

2. How could I view this situation more positively or neutrally?

    _____

    _____

    _____

3. What new belief or mantra could I adopt to counteract this pattern?

    _____

    _____

    _____

For example, consider someone who often thinks, "I'm not good enough." Evidence against this thought might include past achievements, compliments from others, or times they've overcome challenges. Reframing it could lead to a new mantra like, "I am capable and growing every day."

Rewriting your inner narrative helps you replace limiting beliefs with thoughts that empower and uplift you. Together, we'll transform your mindset into one of possibility and growth.

Choose one negative thought pattern and explore how you can reframe it. Answer the following:

1. What is the evidence for and against this thought?

    _____

    _____

    _____

2. How could I view this situation more positively or neutrally?

    _____

    _____

    _____

3. What new belief or mantra could I adopt to counteract this pattern?

    _____

    _____

    _____

Rewriting your inner narrative helps you replace limiting beliefs with thoughts that empower and uplift you. Together, we'll transform your mindset into one of possibility and growth.

Visualization: Breaking the Chain

Close your eyes and imagine a heavy chain wrapped around you, each link representing a negative pattern. Visualize yourself breaking each link, one by one, until you're free. Reflect on how this imagery feels and what it represents for your journey.

Journal Prompt

Write about a time when you successfully overcame a negative thought or pattern. Describe the specific thought or behavior, the moment you decided to address it, and the steps you took to break free. How did this process affect your emotional and mental well-being, both immediately and in the long term? Reflect on how it felt to move forward and the lessons you gained from the experience.

_____

_____

_____

_____

_____

Action Step

Identify one negative pattern and commit to a new response this week. Practice replacing it with a positive thought or action. Each intentional step creates a ripple effect of growth and empowerment.

_____

_____

_____

_____

_____

Chapter

4

Forgiveness is a journey of strength and courage.
Let's walk this path together, one step at a time.

BUILDING RESILIENCE
THROUGH FORGIVENESS

The Power of Letting Go

Forgiveness is one of the most powerful tools for emotional resilience and healing. In Chapter 4, we delve into how holding onto resentment or anger can weigh us down, keeping us tethered to the past. Forgiveness doesn't mean condoning hurtful actions; instead, it's about releasing the hold those actions have on your heart and mind.

When you choose to forgive, you free yourself from the burden of carrying anger, pain, or disappointment. It's not always easy, but the freedom and peace it brings are worth the effort. Studies have shown that forgiveness can have profound physical health benefits, such as reducing stress, lowering blood pressure, and improving sleep quality. For example, letting go of resentment can help your body release tension, leading to more restful nights and increased energy during the day.

Together, we'll explore how forgiveness can transform your life and help you build emotional strength and resilience.

Forgiveness is one of the most powerful tools for emotional resilience and healing. In Chapter 4, we delve into how holding onto resentment or anger can weigh us down, keeping us tethered to the past. Forgiveness doesn't mean condoning hurtful actions; instead, it's about releasing the hold those actions have on your heart and mind.

When you choose to forgive, you free yourself from the burden of carrying anger, pain, or disappointment. It's not always easy, but the freedom and peace it brings are worth the effort. Together, we'll explore how forgiveness can transform your life and help you build emotional strength and resilience.

Exercise 1: Forgiveness Reflection

Think about someone you've struggled to forgive, even if it's yourself. Reflect on the following questions:

1. What emotions come up when you think about this person or situation?

   _____

   _____

   _____

2. How has holding onto these feelings impacted your life?

   _____

   _____

   _____

3. What would it feel like to release this burden and forgive?

_____

_____

_____

This exercise isn't about forcing forgiveness but exploring the possibility of freeing yourself from the grip of resentment. Let's take this journey one step at a time.

Exercise 2: The Letter of Release

Write a letter to the person you're working to forgive, even if you never send it. In your letter, express how their actions affected you and what you're choosing to release. End the letter with a statement of forgiveness, such as, "I release this burden and choose peace."

Writing this letter can be a powerful step in letting go and reclaiming your emotional well-being. After writing, consider reading the letter aloud to yourself. Hearing your own voice affirm the release can help process your emotions and solidify your feelings of forgiveness. Remember, forgiveness is a gift you give yourself.

Write a letter to the person you're working to forgive, even if you never send it. In your letter, express how their actions affected you and what you're choosing to release. End the letter with a statement of forgiveness, such as, "I release this burden and choose peace."

Writing this letter can be a powerful step in letting go and reclaiming your emotional well-being. Remember, forgiveness is a gift you give yourself.

Visualization: Cutting the Cord

Close your eyes and imagine a cord connecting you to the person or situation you're working to forgive. Visualize yourself gently cutting the cord, symbolizing your decision to let go of the emotional attachment. As the cord dissolves, notice the sensations in your body: a lightness in your chest, a deepening of your breath, or a sense of relief washing over you. Feel the weight lift as you reclaim your emotional freedom and clarity. Take a moment to appreciate the newfound space within you, filled with peace and possibility.

Journal Prompt

Reflect on a time when you forgave someone and the impact it had on your life. How did it change your perspective, and what lessons did you learn from the experience?

_____

_____

_____

_____

_____

Action Step

This week, take one small step toward forgiveness. It could be reflecting on the positive outcomes of releasing resentment, writing your letter of release, or simply acknowledging your readiness to let go. Every step brings you closer to freedom and peace.

_____

_____

_____

_____

_____

Chapter

5

Forgiveness is a journey of strength and courage.
Let's walk this path together, one step at a time.

CULTIVATING INNER PEACE THROUGH ACCEPTANCE

The Role of Acceptance in Emotional Freedom

In Chapter 5, we explore the transformative power of acceptance. Acceptance doesn't mean resignation; rather, it's about acknowledging reality without judgment and finding peace within the present moment. For example, acknowledging reality without judgment might involve recognizing that a missed opportunity doesn't define your worth, but simply reflects a moment in time. Instead of labeling the situation as "failure," you accept it as part of your journey, allowing yourself to move forward with clarity and purpose. Many of us carry the burden of resisting what we cannot change, which only deepens our emotional struggles. By embracing acceptance, we open ourselves to healing, clarity, and inner peace. For instance, consider a situation where you've faced unexpected changes at work. Instead of fixating on what could have been, shifting your focus to what's within your control—like developing new skills or seeking support—can foster a sense of empowerment and serenity. This shift in perspective helps you to let go of unnecessary stress and embrace peace in the present moment.

Acceptance invites us to let go of the "what ifs" and "should haves" that keep us tethered to the past or anxious about the future. Instead, it teaches us to focus on what we can control—our thoughts, actions, and perspective. This chapter will guide you through exercises designed to help you cultivate acceptance, release resistance, and step into the freedom of living fully in the now.

Exercise 1: Accepting What Is

Reflect on a situation in your life that you've been resisting. Take a moment to acknowledge the emotions tied to this resistance. Is it fear, frustration, or sadness? These feelings hold clues to understanding your struggle. Answer the following questions:

1. What aspects of this situation are outside of your control?

   _____

   _____

   _____

2. How has resisting this reality affected your emotions and well-being?

   _____

   _____

   _____

3. What would it look like to accept this situation as it is?

   _____

   _____

   _____

Write down one affirmation that reinforces acceptance, such as "I release the need to control what I cannot change."

Exercise 2: Gratitude for the Present Moment

Take a few minutes to sit quietly and reflect on the present moment. Notice your surroundings, the rhythm of your breath, and any sensations in your body, such as warmth, calmness, or tension. Let your awareness settle on the here and now. Write a list of three things you're grateful for right now, no matter how small—a soft breeze, a kind word, or a moment of stillness. Gratitude helps shift your focus from resistance to appreciation, fostering a sense of peace, grounding, and contentment.

Visualization: The Calm River

Close your eyes and imagine a gentle river flowing steadily. Picture yourself placing a small boat into the water, filled with your worries and resistance. Watch as the boat drifts away, carried effortlessly by the current. Feel the tension leaving your body as you let go. Reflect on the calmness and stillness within you.

Journal Prompt

Write about a time when you resisted a situation but later found peace through acceptance. Describe the circumstances surrounding the situation and the emotions you experienced while resisting. How did you ultimately arrive at a place of acceptance? How did your perspective shift, and what positive changes did you notice in your emotional well-being and relationships? Reflect on the lessons you learned from the experience and how they have influenced your current approach to challenges.

_____

_____

_____

_____

_____

Action Step

This week, practice mindful acceptance by identifying one area of your life where you tend to resist. Pay attention to how this resistance manifests—whether it's through tension in your body, repetitive thoughts, or emotional unease. Whenever you feel resistance arise, take a deep breath, repeat your affirmation, and remind yourself that peace comes from within. Use this moment as an opportunity to ground yourself and refocus on the present, reinforcing your commitment to living with clarity and calm.

_____

_____

_____

_____

_____

Chapter 6

Acceptance is a gift of clarity and liberation.
Let's embrace it together, one step at a time.

EMBRACING GROWTH AND CHANGE

The Power of Growth in Your Healing Journey

In Chapter 6, we explore the transformative nature of growth and change. Growth is a natural part of life, but it often feels uncomfortable because it pushes us out of familiar patterns. Yet, it's in those moments of discomfort that we find our greatest opportunities for healing and self-discovery. Change is the catalyst for growth—it helps us shed what no longer serves us and step into new possibilities.

Embracing growth doesn't mean having all the answers; it means being willing to ask the questions, try new approaches, and take small, consistent steps forward. Whether it's overcoming fears, learning new skills, or creating healthier habits, growth requires patience, persistence, and a commitment to your well-being.

This chapter will guide you through exercises and reflections to help you navigate change with confidence and harness its potential to transform your life. Together, we'll embrace growth as an integral part of your journey to freedom.

Exercise 1: Reflecting on Growth Opportunities

Think about a time when change led to personal growth. Answer the following questions:

1. What was the situation, and how did it initially feel?

   _____

   _____

   _____

2. What steps did you take to adapt to the change?

   _____

   _____

   _____

3. What positive outcomes came from the experience?

   _____

   _____

   _____

Now, consider an area of your life where growth feels needed. Reflect on how embracing change in this area could positively impact your well-being.

Exercise 2: Setting Growth Goals

Choose one area of your life where you want to grow—whether it's emotionally, professionally, spiritually, or physically. Answer the following:

1. What specific change do you want to make?

   _____

   _____

   _____

2. What steps can you take to move toward this goal?

   _____

   _____

   _____

3. What potential challenges might arise, and how can you address them?

   _____

   _____

   _____

Write down a small, actionable goal for this week that aligns with your desired growth. Commit to taking one step, no matter how small, to move forward.

Visualization: Blooming Through Change

Close your eyes and imagine yourself as a seed planted in fertile soil. Picture yourself growing roots, drawing strength from the earth, and reaching upward toward the light. Visualize each stage of growth as you overcome challenges and thrive. Reflect on how this imagery represents your capacity for transformation and renewal.

Journal Prompt

Write about a change you're currently facing or anticipating. What fears or doubts come up when you think about this change? How can you reframe these thoughts to see the growth opportunities within the challenge?

_____

_____

_____

_____

_____

Action Step

This week, embrace one small change. Whether it's trying a new habit, stepping out of your comfort zone, or simply shifting your perspective, take a step toward growth. Celebrate the effort, knowing that each step brings you closer to becoming the person you're meant to be.

_____

_____

_____

_____

_____

Chapter 7

Growth is a journey, not a destination.
Let's embrace each step with courage and grace

BUILDING A LIFE OF PURPOSE AND FULFILLMENT

Discovering Your Purpose

In Chapter 7, we turn our focus toward living a life of purpose and fulfillment. Purpose gives our lives meaning, direction, and motivation. Without it, we often feel adrift, unsure of our next steps. Discovering your purpose is not about finding one definitive answer—it's about exploring your passions, values, and the ways you want to make an impact in the world.

A purposeful life is built on intentional choices and meaningful actions. It's about aligning your daily life with what truly matters to you. Whether your purpose is rooted in your family, career, community, or personal growth, uncovering it allows you to live with clarity and conviction.

This chapter will guide you through exercises and reflections to help you identify and cultivate your sense of purpose. Together, we'll create a roadmap to a more fulfilling life.

Exercise 1: Identifying Your Values

Your values are the foundation of your purpose. Reflect on the following questions:

1. What are the three most important things in your life right now?

   _____

   _____

   _____

2. When do you feel the most fulfilled or alive?

   _____

   _____

   _____

3. What do you want to be remembered for?

   _____

   _____

   _____

Write down your answers and look for themes that resonate deeply. These values will guide you as you build a life of purpose.

Exercise 2: Crafting a Vision Statement

Think about the kind of life you want to create. Answer the following:

1. How do you want to spend your time and energy?

   _____

   _____

   _____

2. Who do you want to impact, and in what way?

_____

_____

_____

3. What legacy do you want to leave behind?

_____

_____

_____

Using your answers, write a personal vision statement. For example, "I want to create a life where I uplift others through compassion, lead with integrity, and inspire positive change." Keep this statement somewhere you can revisit it often.

Visualization: Walking the Path of Purpose

Close your eyes and picture yourself on a path lined with opportunities and challenges. Imagine yourself walking confidently, guided by your values and passions. See yourself reaching milestones and celebrating moments of fulfillment. Reflect on the strength and clarity you feel as you move toward your purpose.

Journal Prompt

Write about a time when you felt truly fulfilled or purposeful. What were you doing, and why did it feel meaningful? How can you incorporate more of this into your life moving forward?

_____

_____

_____

_____

_____

Action Step

This week, take one intentional action that aligns with your purpose. Whether it's reaching out to someone who inspires you, starting a new project, or dedicating time to something you love, make a choice that reflects the life you want to build.

_____

_____

_____

_____

_____

Chapter 8

Living with purpose is a journey of discovery, intention, and impact. Let's take the next step together.

CREATING A LEGACY OF LOVE AND IMPACT

What Legacy Will You Leave?

In Chapter 8, we explore the idea of legacy—the lasting imprint we leave on the lives we touch and the world around us. A legacy is not just about material wealth or accomplishments; it's about the values, love, and lessons we pass on to others. It's the ripple effect of our actions, words, and intentions.

Creating a meaningful legacy starts with living intentionally today. When you align your choices with the impact you want to leave behind, you inspire others and create a life that reflects your deepest values. Your legacy is built in the everyday moments, the relationships you nurture, and the kindness you show.

This chapter will guide you through exercises that help you define the legacy you want to leave and the steps you can take to live in alignment with that vision. Together, we'll explore how to create a life of love, purpose, and enduring impact.

Exercise 1: Defining Your Legacy

Reflect on the following questions:

1. What do you want people to remember most about you?

   _____

   _____

   _____

2. What values do you want to pass on to the next generation?

   _____

   _____

   _____

3. How do your daily actions reflect the legacy you want to leave?

   _____

   _____

   _____

Write your thoughts and consider how your current choices align with your desired legacy.

Exercise 2: Acts of Kindness

Legacy is often built through small, intentional actions. This week, focus on acts of kindness. Answer the following:

1. Who in your life could benefit from your support, encouragement, or love?

   _____

   _____

   _____

2. What small act can you do today to brighten someone else's life?

_____

_____

_____

3. How do you feel after performing an act of kindness?

_____

_____

_____

Record your experiences and reflect on how these actions contribute to your legacy.

Visualization: Planting Seeds of Love

Close your eyes and imagine planting seeds in a beautiful garden. Each seed represents an action, value, or relationship you've nurtured. Visualize these seeds growing into vibrant flowers and trees, representing the positive impact you've had on others. Reflect on the beauty of your garden and the legacy it symbolizes.

Journal Prompt

Write about someone whose legacy has deeply impacted your life. What did they teach you, and how has their influence shaped who you are today? How can you honor their legacy through your own actions?

_____

_____

_____

_____

Action Step

This week, choose one action that represents the legacy you want to leave. It could be writing a heartfelt letter, mentoring someone, or volunteering for a cause you care about. Take this step as a way to live intentionally and inspire others.

_____

_____

_____

_____

_____

A meaningful legacy is built one moment, one choice, and one connection at a time. Let's create yours together.

EMPOWERING OTHERS THROUGH YOUR JOURNEY

The Ripple Effect of Empowerment

In Chapter 9, we explore how your healing and growth can empower others. Every step you take toward emotional freedom, resilience, and purpose creates a ripple effect, inspiring those around you to embark on their own journeys. Empowerment isn't about fixing others; it's about sharing your story, offering support, and leading by example.

When you choose to be open about your experiences, you foster connection, understanding, and hope. Your journey can be a source of strength for someone else who may feel stuck or uncertain. This chapter will guide you in identifying ways to empower others through your growth, helping you become a beacon of encouragement and positivity in their lives.

Exercise 1: Reflecting on Your Influence

Consider how your journey has impacted those around you. Answer the following:

1. Who in your life has noticed changes in you since you began this process?

   _____

   _____

   _____

2. How have your actions, words, or mindset shifts inspired them?

   _____

   _____

   _____

3. What aspects of your journey do you feel most proud to share?

   _____

   _____

   _____

Write down your reflections and think about how your story might empower others to take their own steps toward healing and growth.

Exercise 2: Sharing Your Story

Choose one aspect of your journey to share with someone who might benefit from hearing it. Answer the following:

1. What part of your story could provide encouragement or hope?

    _____

    _____

    _____

2. How can you share it in a way that feels authentic and supportive?

    _____

    _____

    _____

3. What response do you hope to inspire in the listener?

    _____

    _____

    _____

Take the opportunity to connect with someone by sharing your experience, whether through a conversation, a written letter, or a social media post.

Visualization: Spreading Light

Close your eyes and imagine yourself holding a small candle in a dark room. As you light other candles around you, the room becomes brighter and warmer. Visualize this light spreading as others pass the flame to those around them, creating a ripple effect of hope and empowerment. Reflect on the power of your light and its ability to inspire change.

Journal Prompt

Write about a time when someone else's story inspired you to take action. What did their journey teach you, and how did it impact your own path? How can you now be that source of inspiration for someone else?

_____

_____

_____

_____

_____

Action Step

This week, take one intentional action to empower someone in your life. It could be offering words of encouragement, sharing a resource, or simply being a compassionate listener. Small actions can create lasting impacts.

_____

_____

_____

_____

_____

Chapter 10

Empowerment is about passing the torch of hope, healing, and growth. Let's light the way for others together.

LIVING FULLY AND AUTHENTICALLY

Embracing Your True Self

In Chapter 10, we focus on living fully and authentically—a culmination of all the work you've done in your healing journey. Living authentically means embracing who you are at your core, free from the weight of emotional baggage or the constraints of societal expectations. It's about aligning your actions with your values, embracing your strengths and imperfections, and showing up as your true self in every aspect of life.

When you live authentically, you experience a deeper sense of freedom and joy. You no longer feel the need to perform or hide but can stand confidently in your truth. This chapter will guide you through exercises and reflections to help you step into the fullness of who you are and live a life that feels true to you.

Exercise 1: Recognizing Your Authentic Self

Reflect on the following questions to uncover your authentic self:

1. When do you feel most like yourself?

   _____

   _____

   _____

2. What qualities or traits make you unique?

   _____

   _____

   _____

3. What fears or doubts hold you back from fully expressing yourself?

   _____

   _____

   _____

Write down your reflections and consider how you can celebrate and amplify these qualities in your daily life.

Exercise 2: Aligning Actions with Values

Authenticity thrives when your actions align with your values. Answer the following:

1. What are three core values that guide your life?

   _____

   _____

   _____

2. Are there areas where your actions don't align with these values?

_____

_____

_____

3. What specific changes can you make to live in greater alignment?

_____

_____

_____

Set one small goal this week to align your actions with your values and take a step toward living authentically.

Visualization: Your Authentic Light

Close your eyes and imagine a warm, radiant light within you. Picture this light expanding with each breath, filling you with confidence and peace. Visualize this light shining outward, illuminating the path ahead and touching those around you. Reflect on the strength and beauty of living authentically.

Journal Prompt

Write about a time when you felt completely authentic and free. What were you doing, and how did it feel? How can you create more opportunities to experience that freedom in your daily life?

_____

_____

_____

_____

_____

Action Step

This week, take one bold action that reflects your authentic self. Whether it's speaking your truth, pursuing a passion, or setting a boundary, make a choice that honors who you are. Celebrate the courage it takes to show up fully and authentically.

_____

_____

_____

_____

Authenticity is your greatest strength. Embrace it,
and let the world see the beauty of your true self.

LIVING BAGGAGE FREE WORKBOOK THE JOURNEY AHEAD

A Final Word of Encouragement

Congratulations on completing the *Living Baggage Free Workbook*! This is not just the end of a workbook—it's the beginning of a transformed life. By taking the time to reflect, engage in the exercises, and commit to your growth, you've taken powerful steps toward emotional freedom, healing, and authenticity.

Remember, healing is a journey, not a destination. There will be moments when the work feels challenging, and that's okay. Give yourself grace, celebrate your progress, and stay open to the lessons along the way. Each step you take moves you closer to a life of clarity, peace, and purpose.

This workbook is a tool you can return to again and again. As life evolves, so will your understanding of yourself and your journey. Feel free to revisit the exercises, reflect on your growth, and continue building the life you deserve.

Healing is a Lifelong Process

Healing doesn't happen overnight—it's an ongoing journey. Every small step you take creates a ripple effect, leading to greater peace and clarity over time. Be patient with yourself and trust the process. Healing isn't about perfection; it's about progress. Let this workbook remind you that your commitment to growth is an act of courage and self-love.

ABOUT THE AUTHOR

Fausta C. Phelan is a transformational author, speaker, and executive leadership coach with a passion for helping individuals break free from emotional baggage. A former military professional and certified Maxwell Leadership Team coach, Fausta combines discipline, compassion, and practical tools to guide others toward healing, resilience, and freedom.

Her book, *Living Baggage Free*, is a powerful guide for those ready to release the weight of their past and step into a life of clarity, peace, and purpose. Fausta's expertise as a DISC consultant and leadership mentor empowers readers to embrace their journey with actionable steps and renewed hope.

Services Offered by Fausta Phelan

Your healing journey doesn't have to end here. Fausta offers personalized support to help you continue your transformation. Explore the following services:

- **One-on-One Coaching**: Personalized sessions to help you navigate challenges and embrace emotional freedom.

- **Mastermind Groups**: Join a supportive community of like-minded individuals working toward growth and healing.

- **Workshops and Events**: Interactive sessions designed to deepen your understanding and application of emotional resilience principles.

To learn more, visit FaustaPhelan.com.

Resources for Further Growth

Continue your journey with these recommended resources:

- Books, articles, and tools referenced in *Living Baggage Free* to support your healing journey.

- Guided meditations, journaling prompts, and practical exercises to reinforce what you've learned.

Gratitude and Next Steps

Thank you for trusting me to guide you on this journey. Remember, you are not alone. Your commitment to healing and growth is an inspiration, and I hope this workbook serves as a lasting resource in your life.

As a final step, I invite you to write a letter to yourself reflecting on your journey through this workbook. Include:

- The most significant insights you've gained.

- The areas where you've grown the most.

- Your hopes and intentions for the future.

Seal this letter and revisit it in six months or a year to reflect on your progress.

If you're ready to take the next step, explore my coaching programs, join a mastermind, or connect with me through my website. I'd be honored to support you further.

Visit FaustaPhelan.com to learn more and continue your journey.

Thank you for trusting me to guide you on this journey. Remember, you are not alone. Your commitment to healing and growth is an inspiration, and I hope this workbook serves as a lasting resource in your life.

If you're ready to take the next step, explore my coaching programs, join a mastermind, or connect with me through my website. I'd be honored to support you further.

Visit FaustaPhelan.com to learn more and continue your journey.